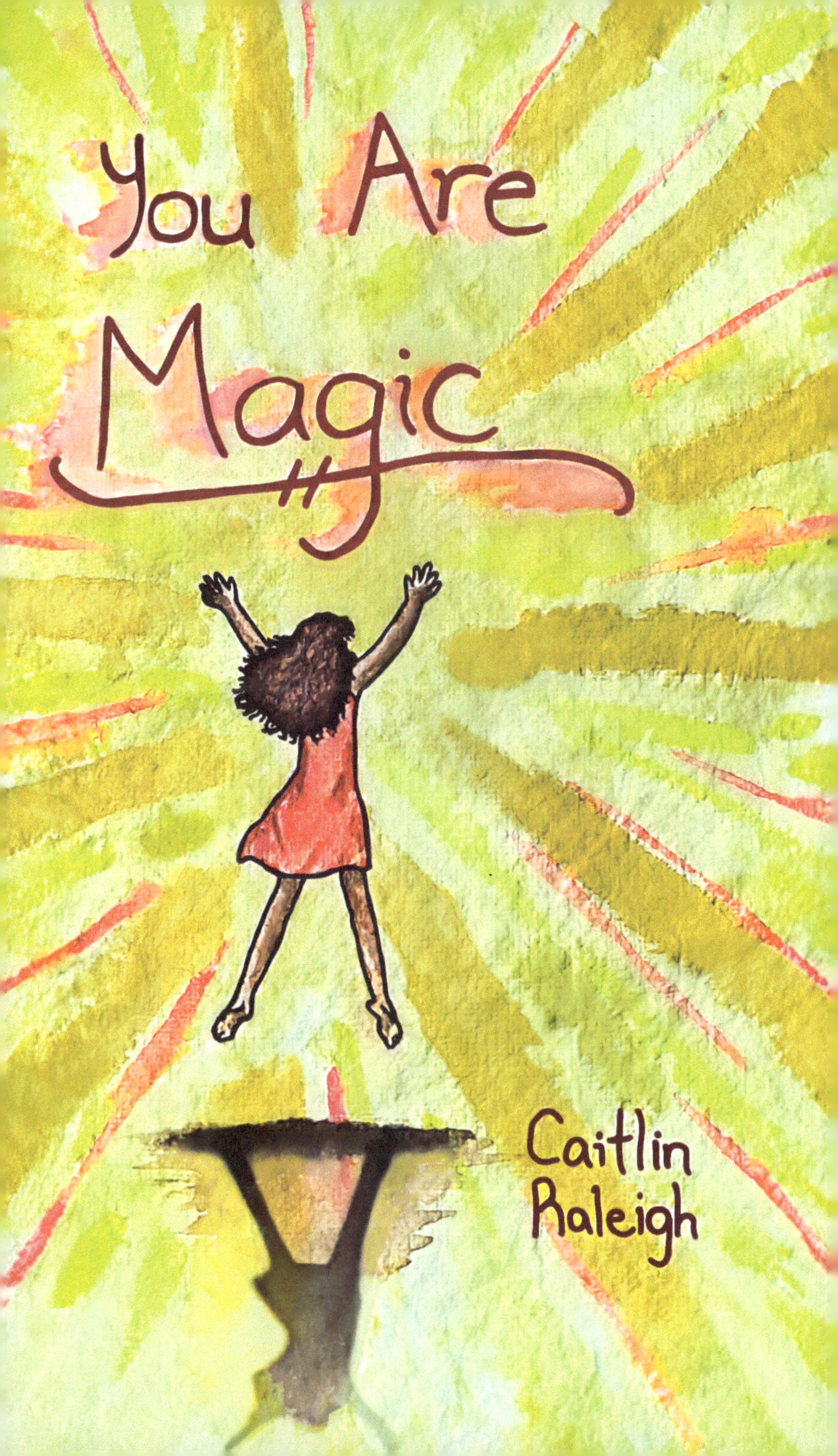
You Are Magic
Caitlin Raleigh

For Veronica Varlow and the NOLA 13, without whom this book would not exist.

For Mom and Dad, without whom I wouldn't be here.

And for Nikki Falk, without whom I wouldn't be me.

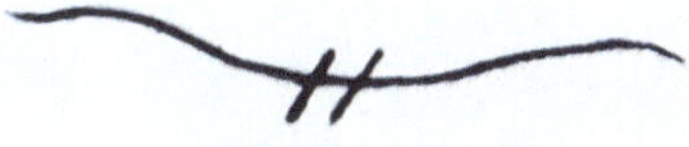 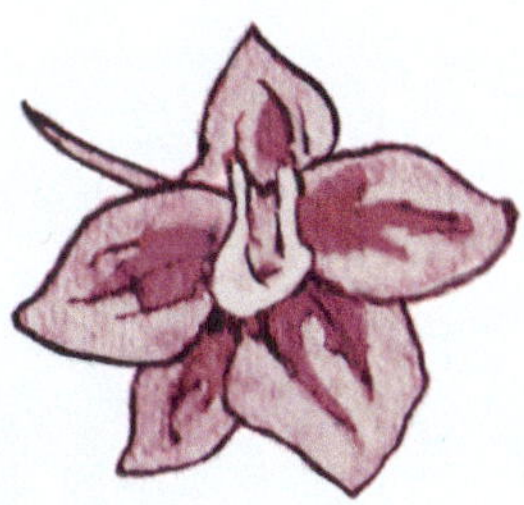

I have a secret to tell you.

You must promise to
keep this secret safe.

Do you promise?

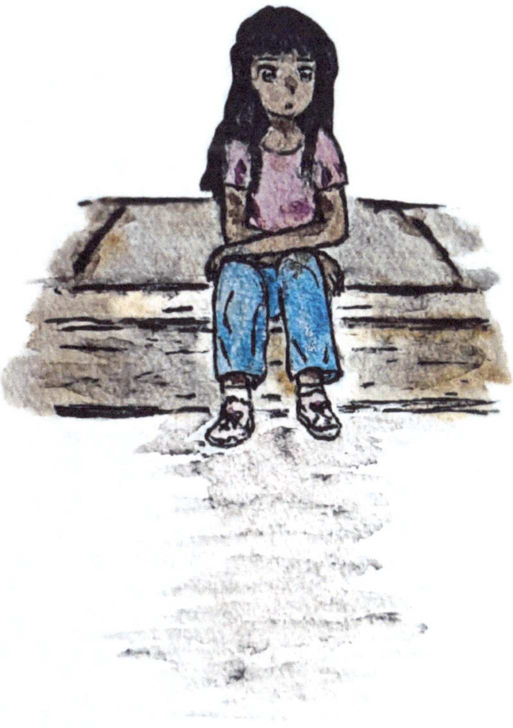

The secret
is this:

you have
magic.

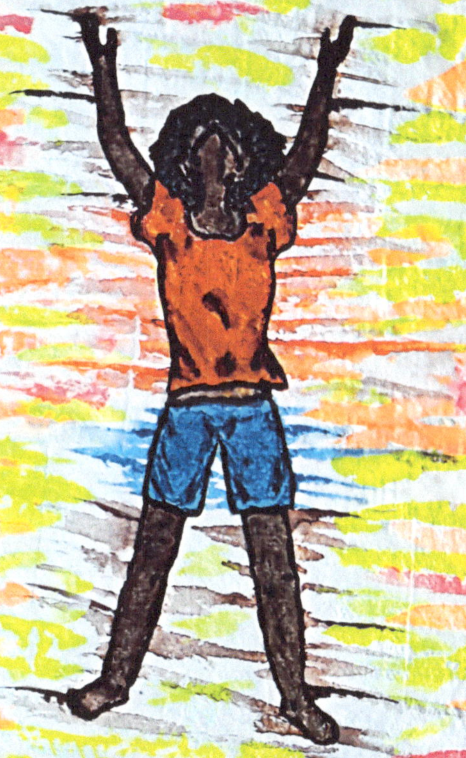

Only you have this unique magic—
no one else in the world.

Maybe you already know what your magic is.

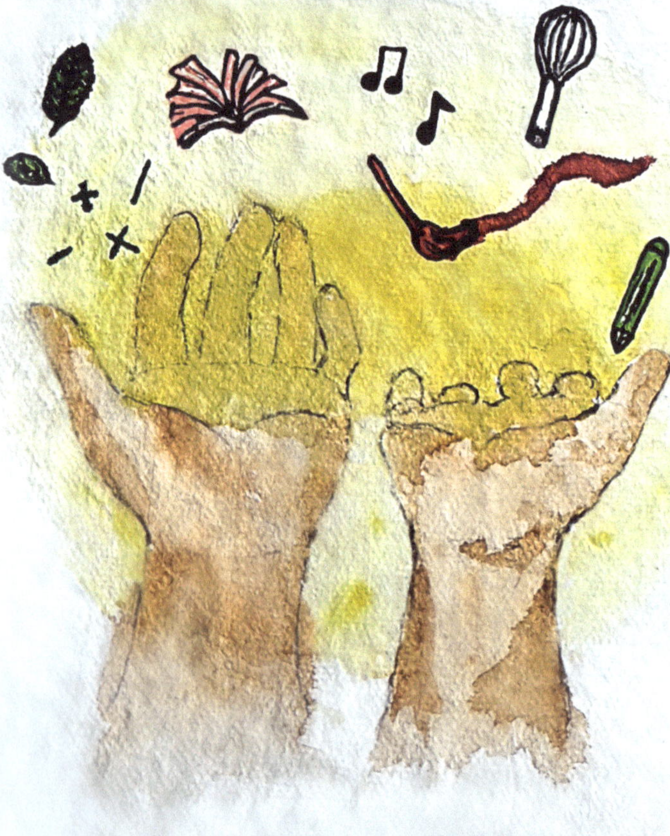

Do you?

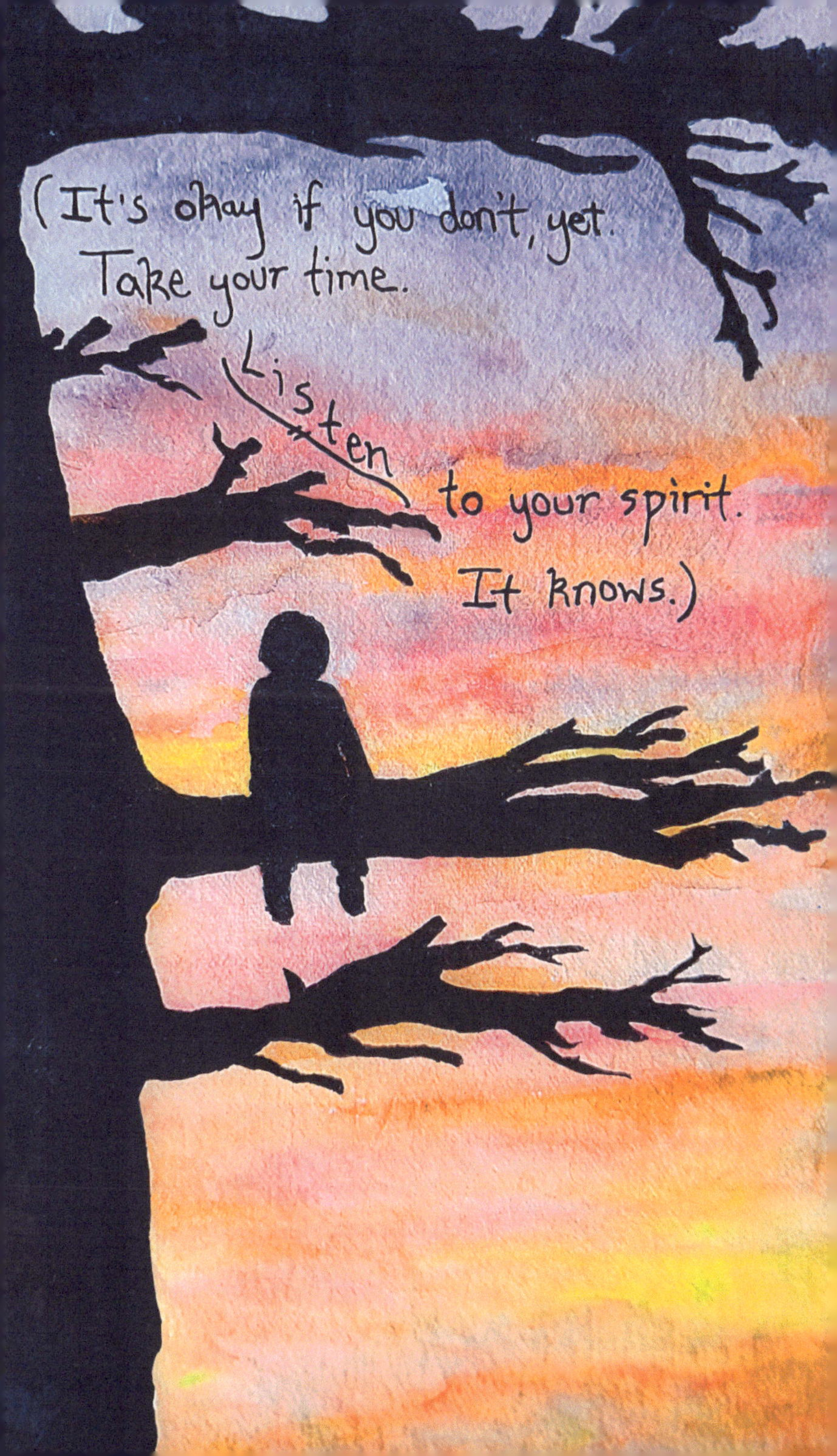
(It's okay if you don't, yet.
Take your time.
Listen
to your spirit.
It knows.)

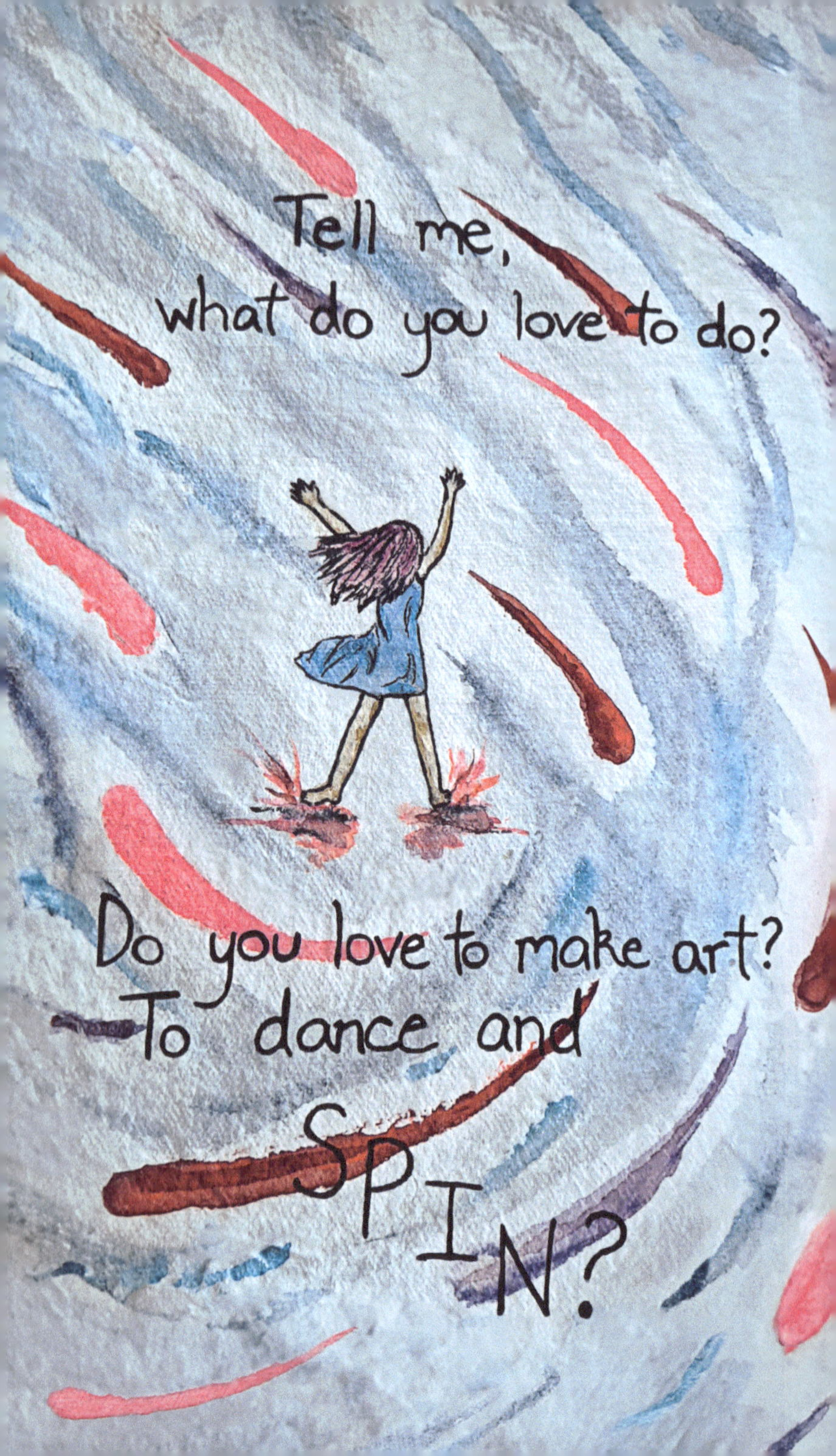
Tell me,
what do you love to do?
Do you love to make art?
To dance and
SPIN?

Do you love to SING,

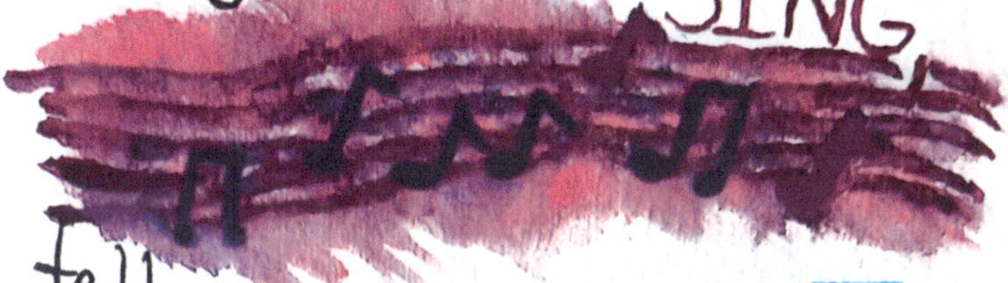

tell STORIES,

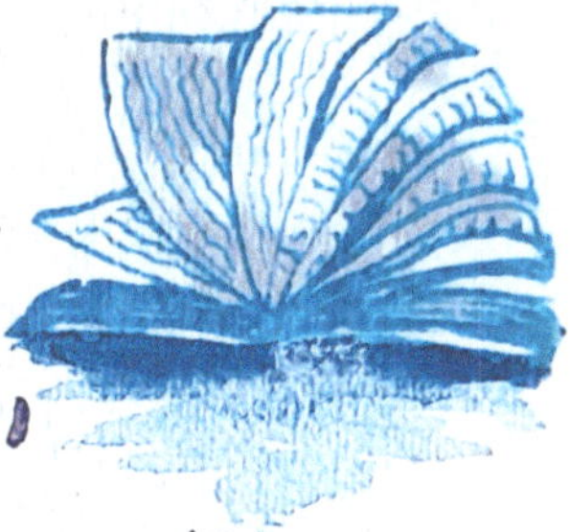

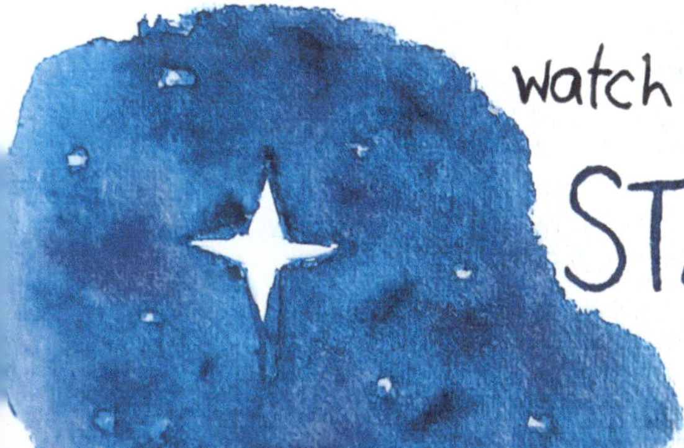

watch the STARS?

What fills you up and makes you happier than ANYTHING?

Your JOY is
a map to your
life's treasure—

what you are
meant to do
in this world.

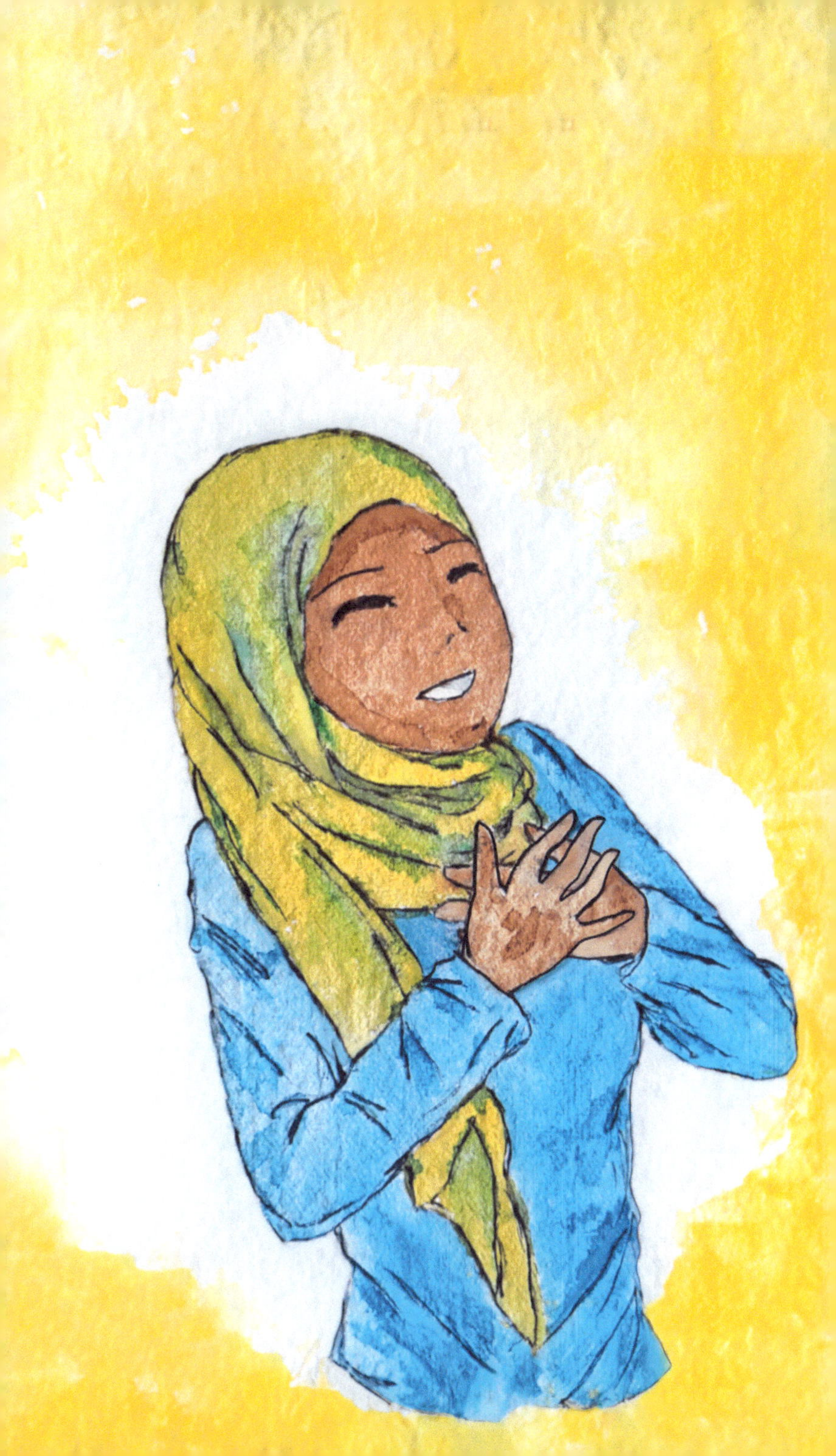

Now, listen:

Not everyone

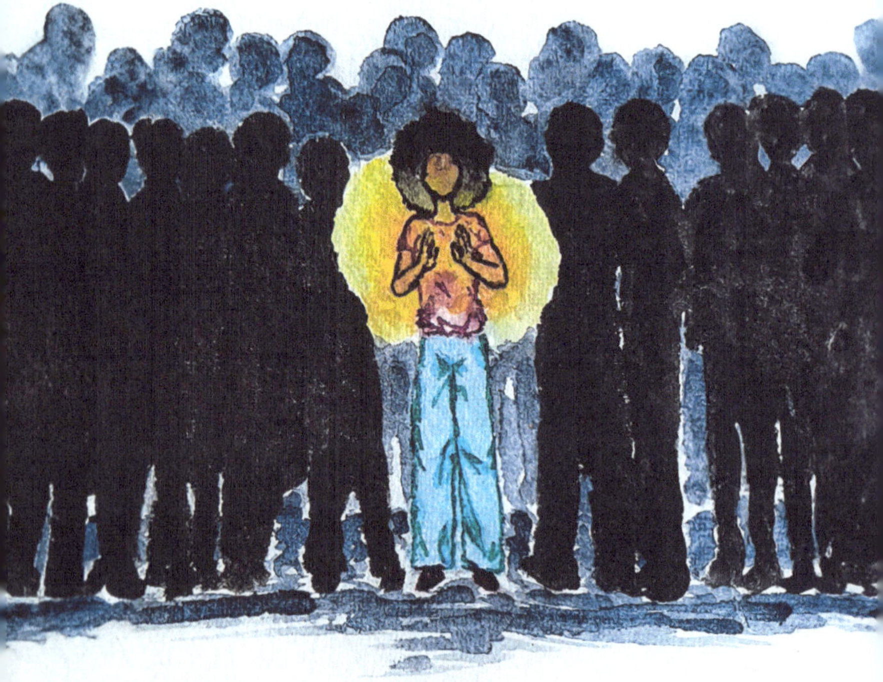

will see your magic
for what it is.

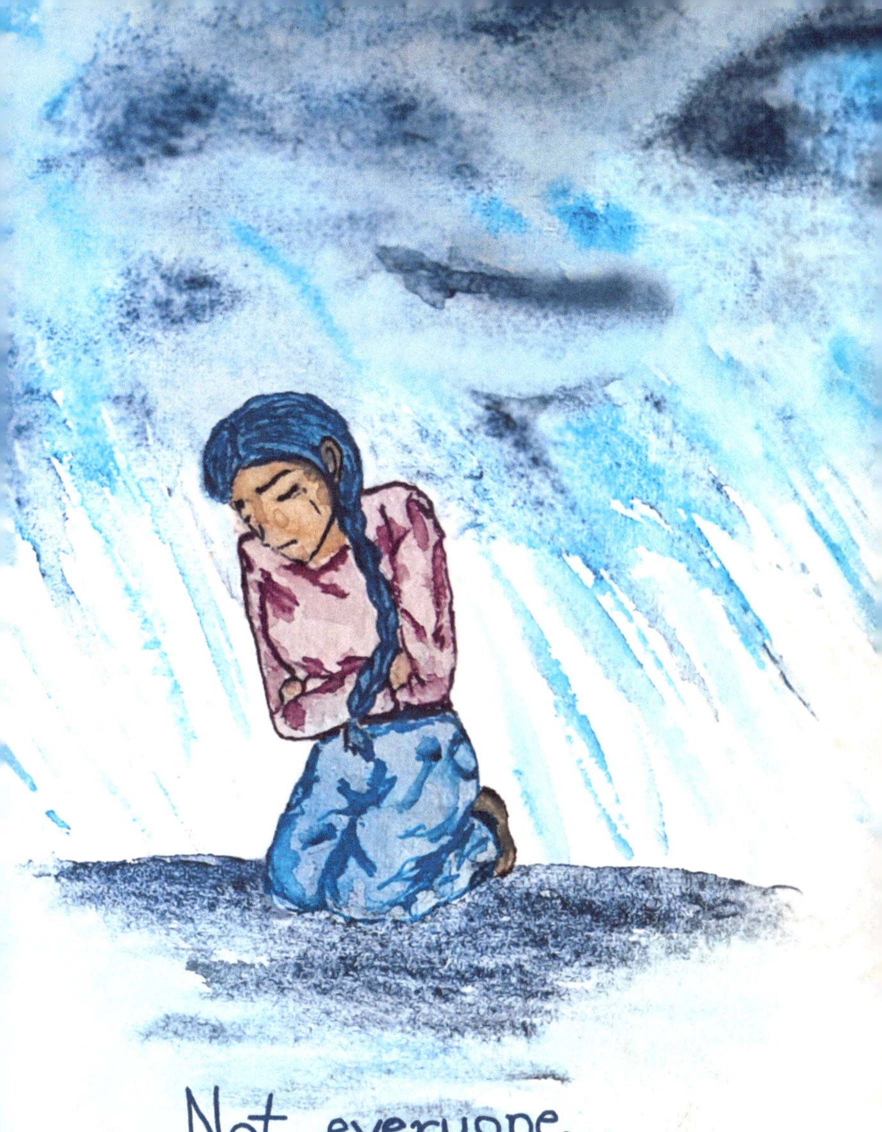

Not everyone
will treat you like the
radiant being you are.

(Sometimes people are
afraid of what it means
to have magic.

And sometimes,

they are afraid they might
not have any themselves.)

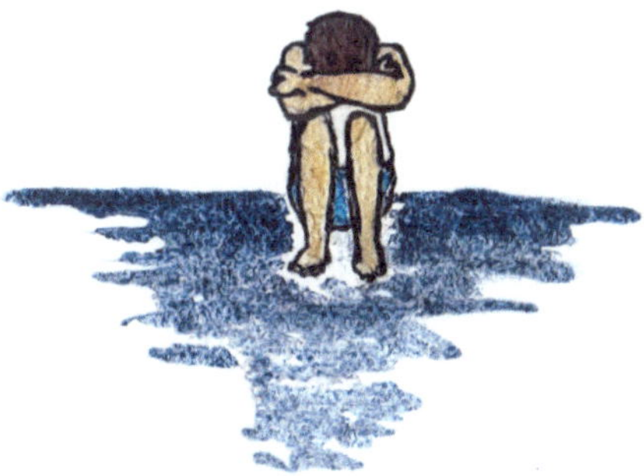

That is why you must
protect its steady fire.

Keep it in your
pocket

and take
it out

whenever
you need t
remember
that it's
there.

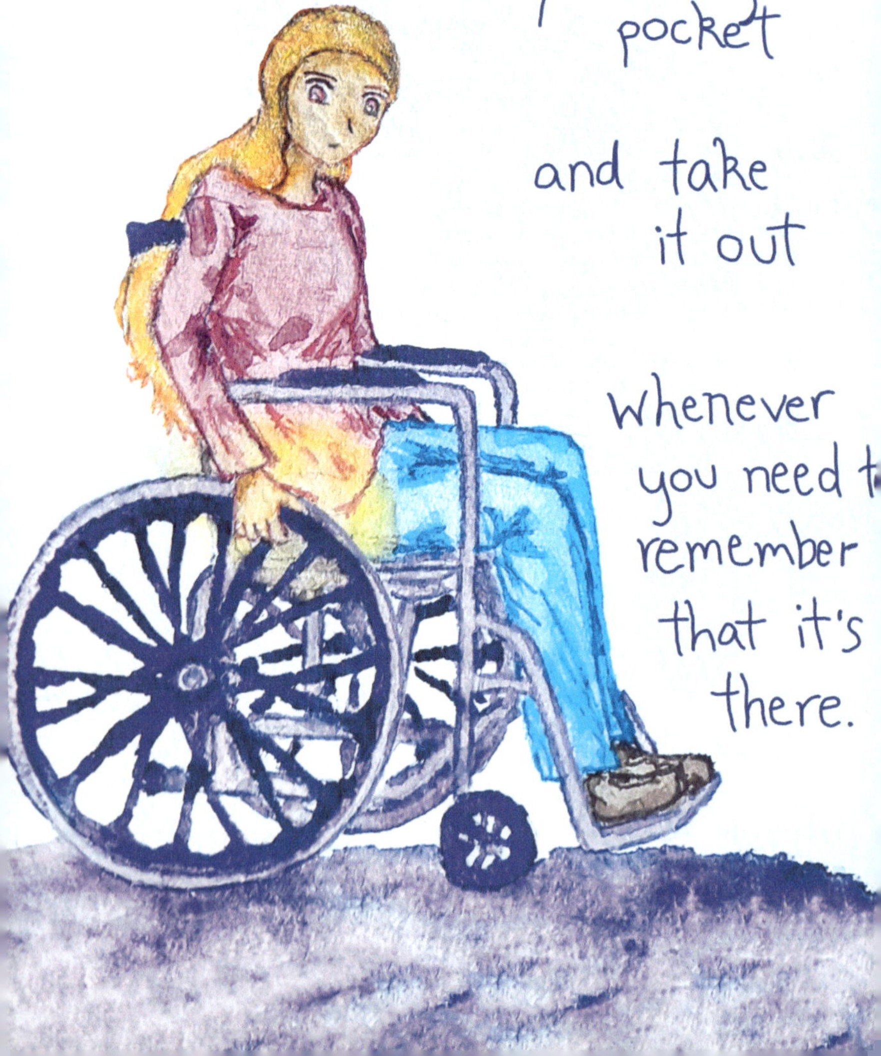

Listen when your magic speaks.

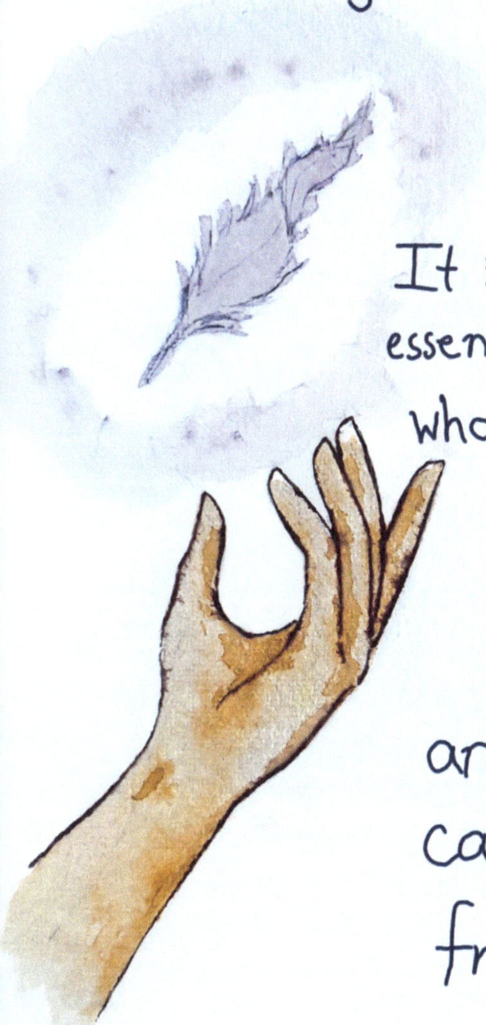

It is the most
essential part of
who you are,

and no one
can take it
from you.

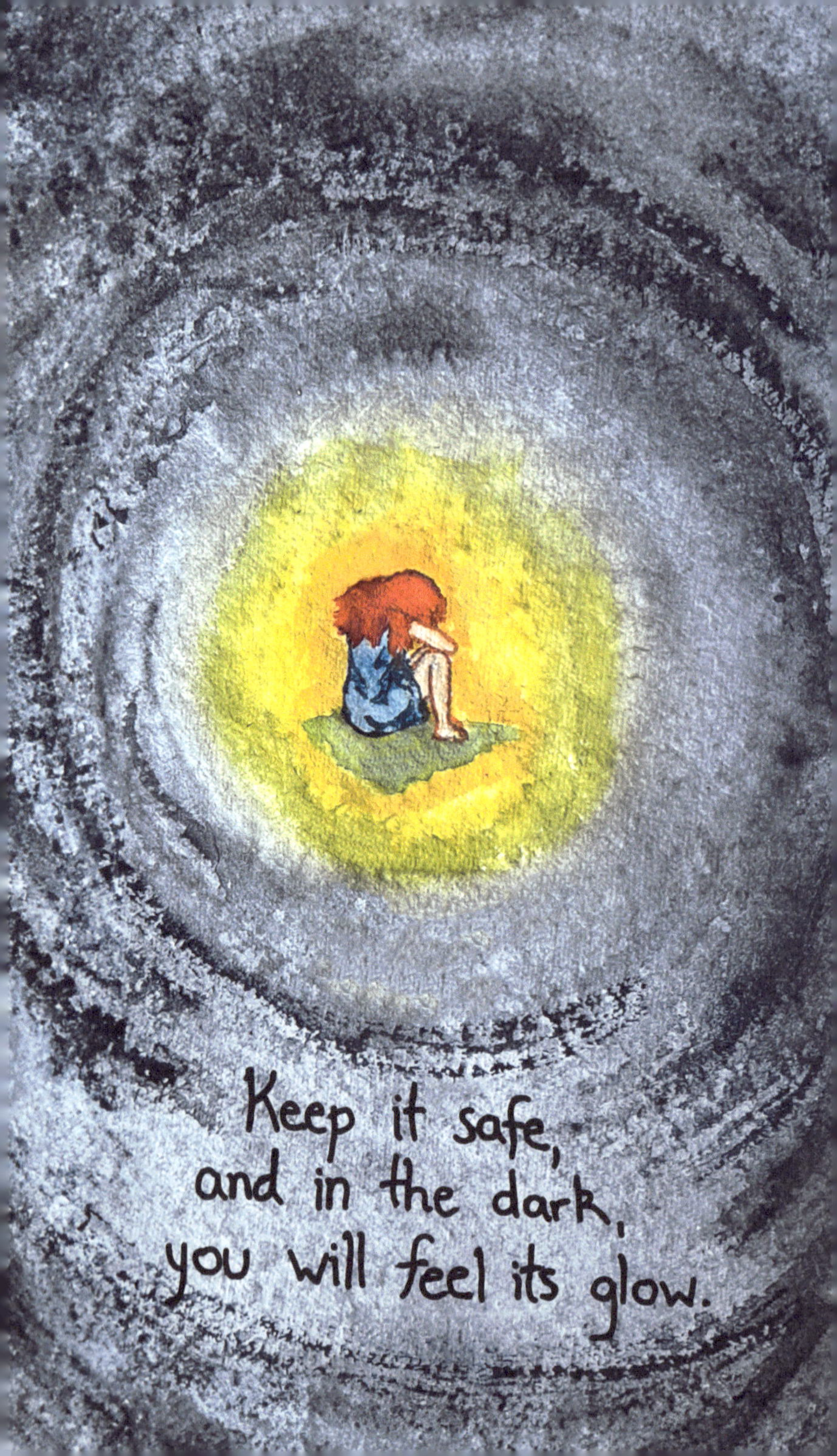
Keep it safe,
and in the dark,
you will feel its glow.

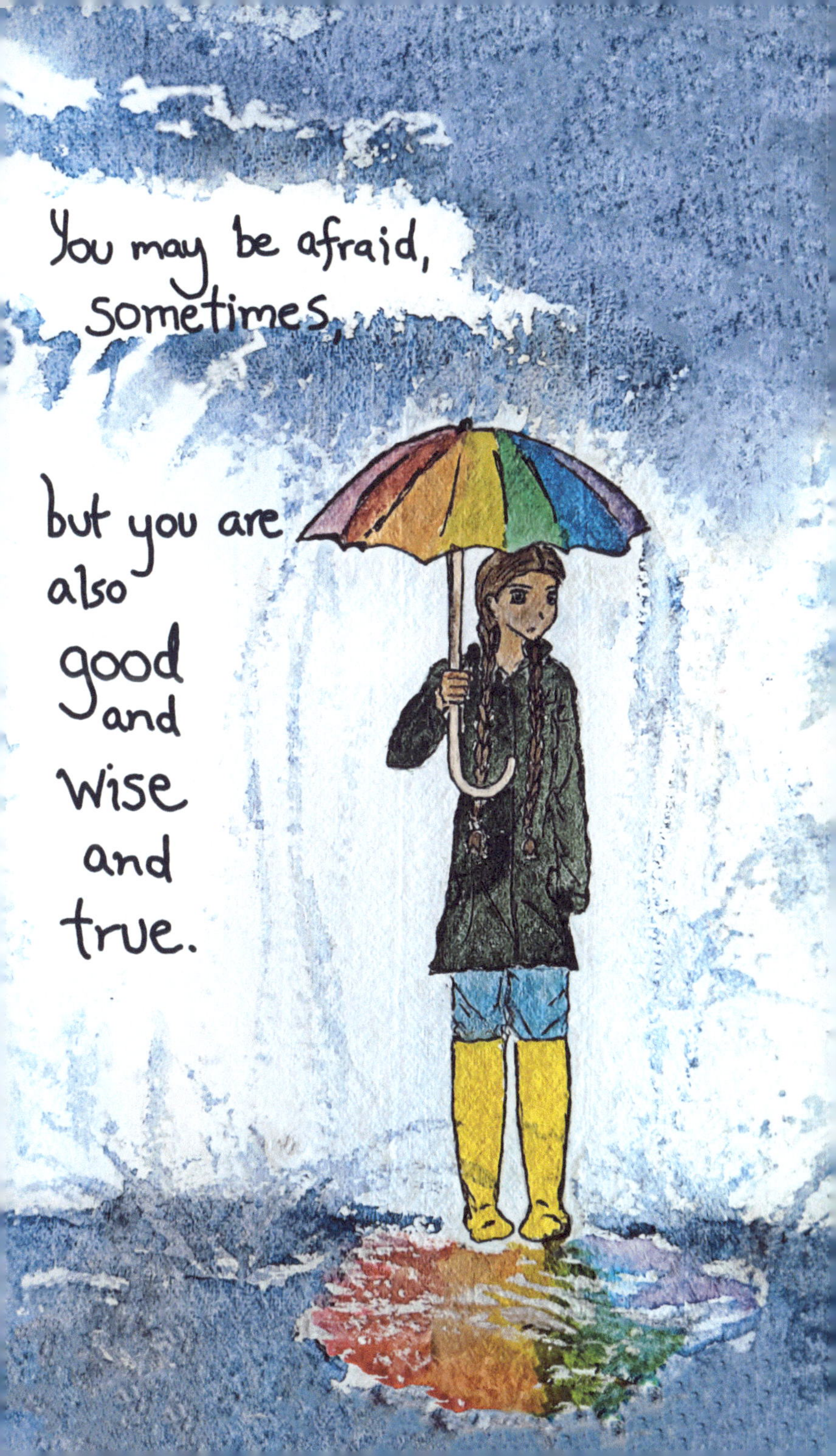
You may be afraid,
sometimes,
but you are
also
good
and
wise
and
true.

Now more than ever,

we need you to shine

BRIGHT

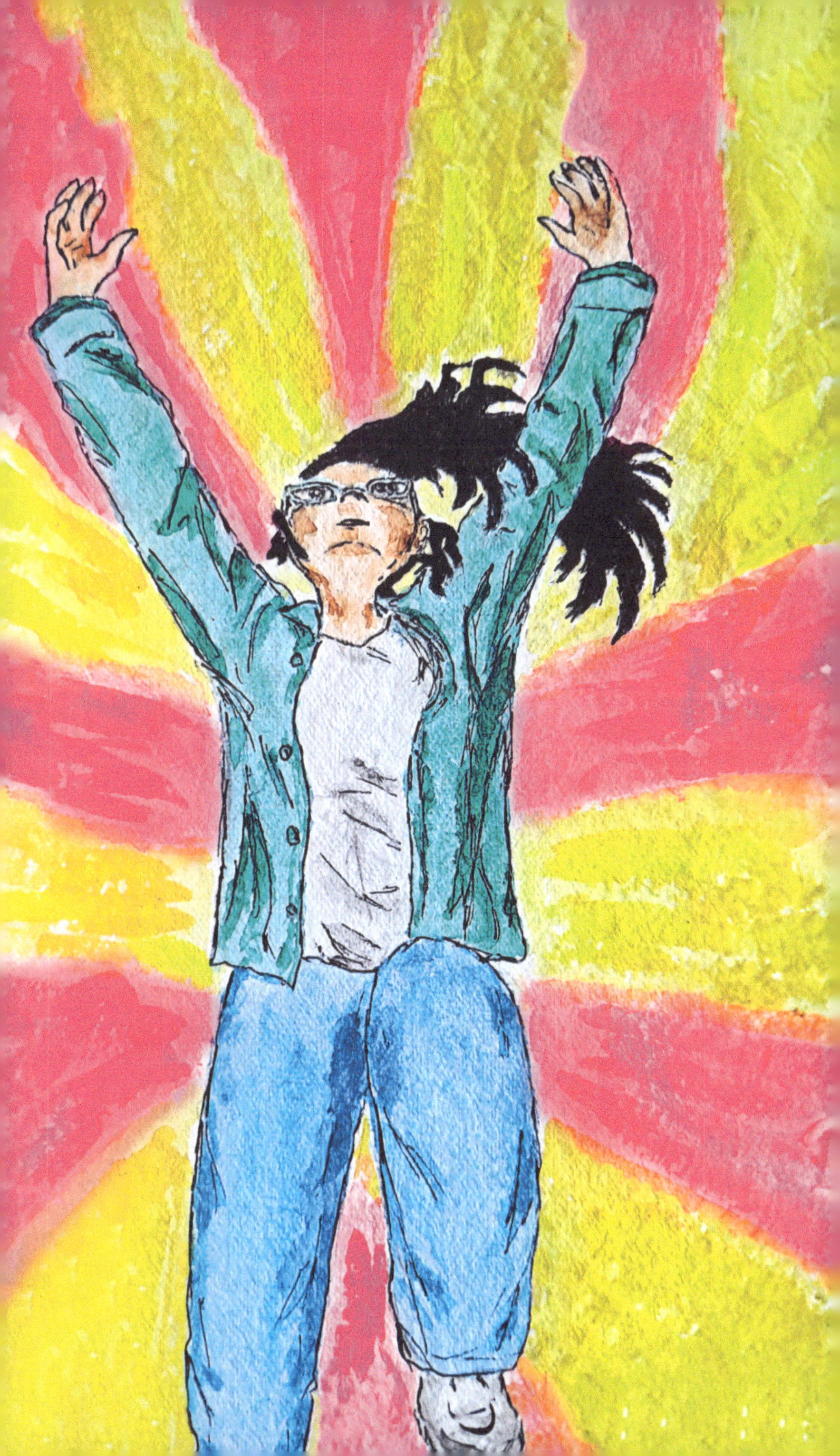

And when you
feel like
your light has
gone out,

Come and sit
with me a while,
my love.

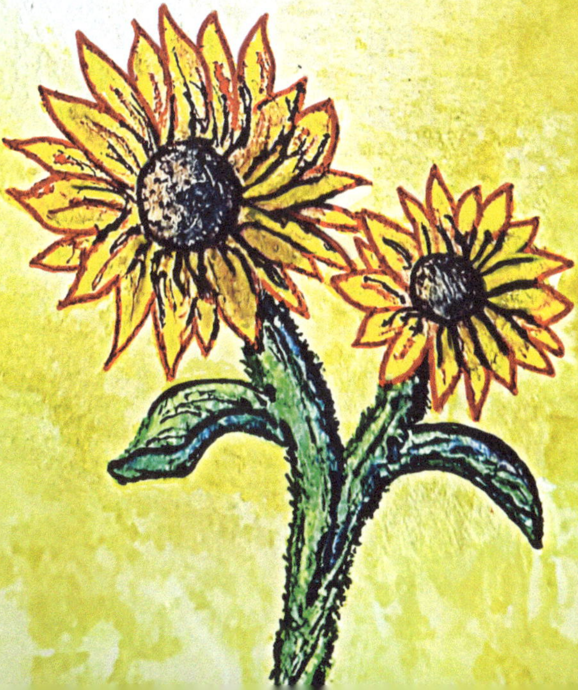

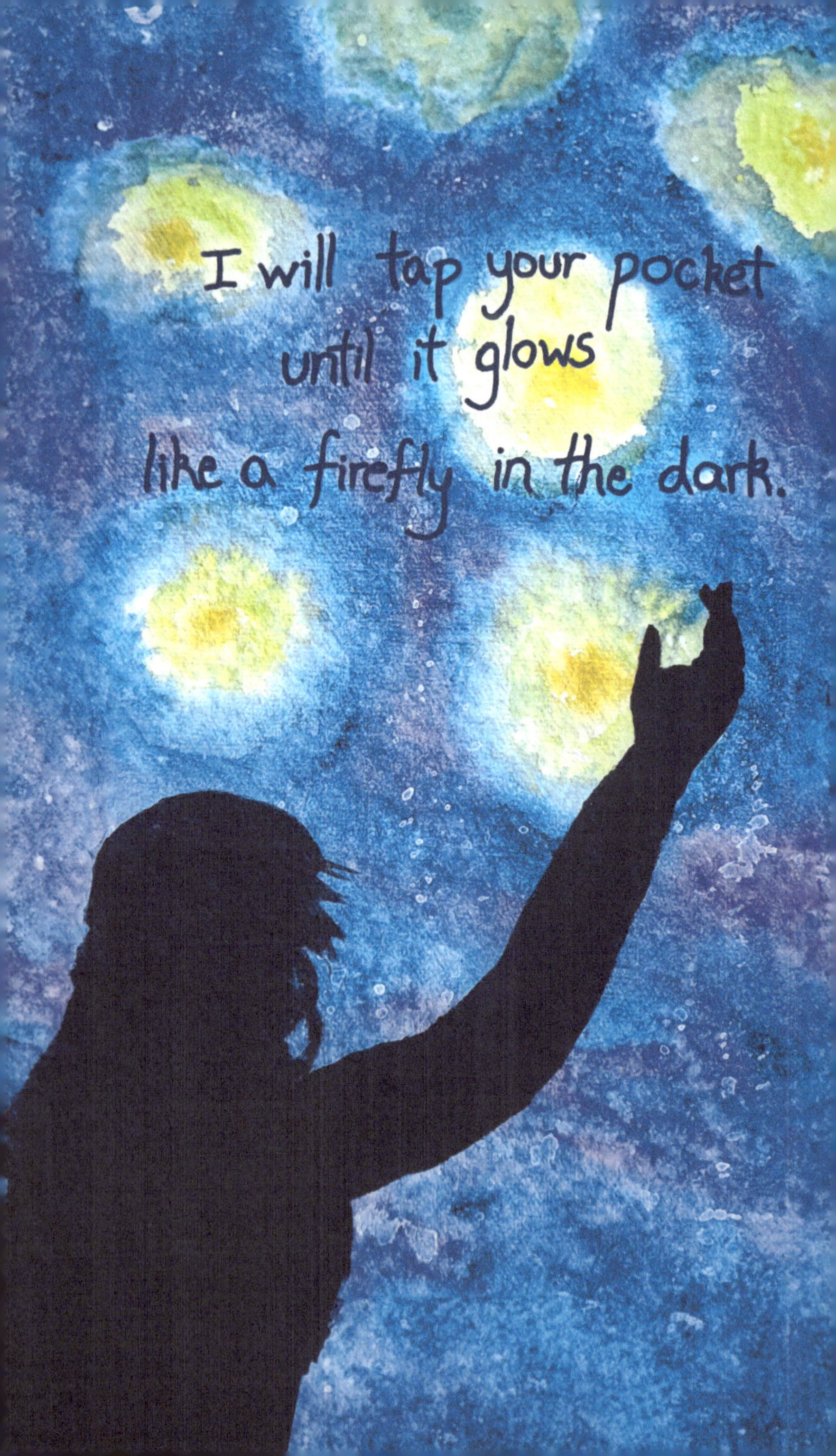
I will tap your pocket
until it glows
like a firefly in the dark.

I'll weave wildflowers
into your hair
and sing your magic bright
again.

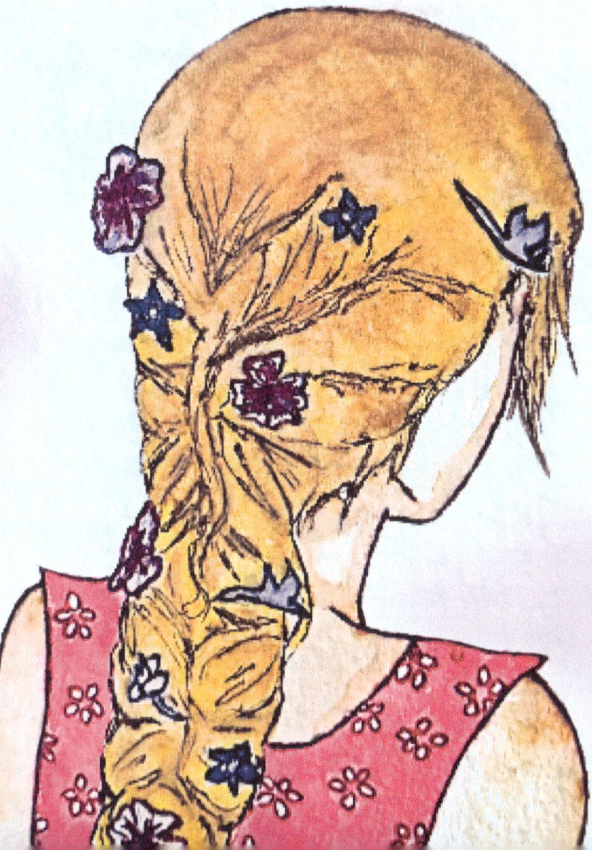

I will

tell you:

You are
precious
and
full of power,
and we can't do
without you.

You can stay here and cry for as long as you need to.

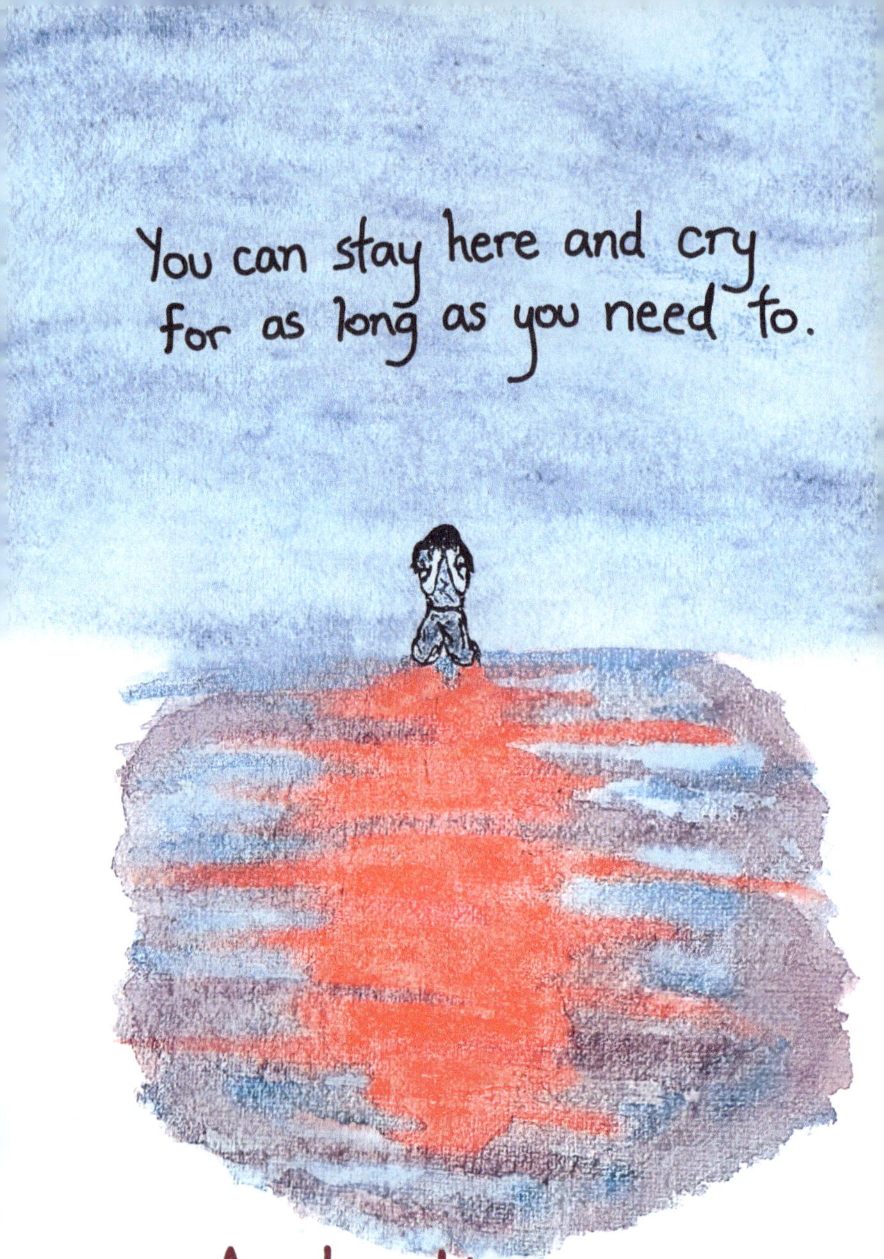

And then—

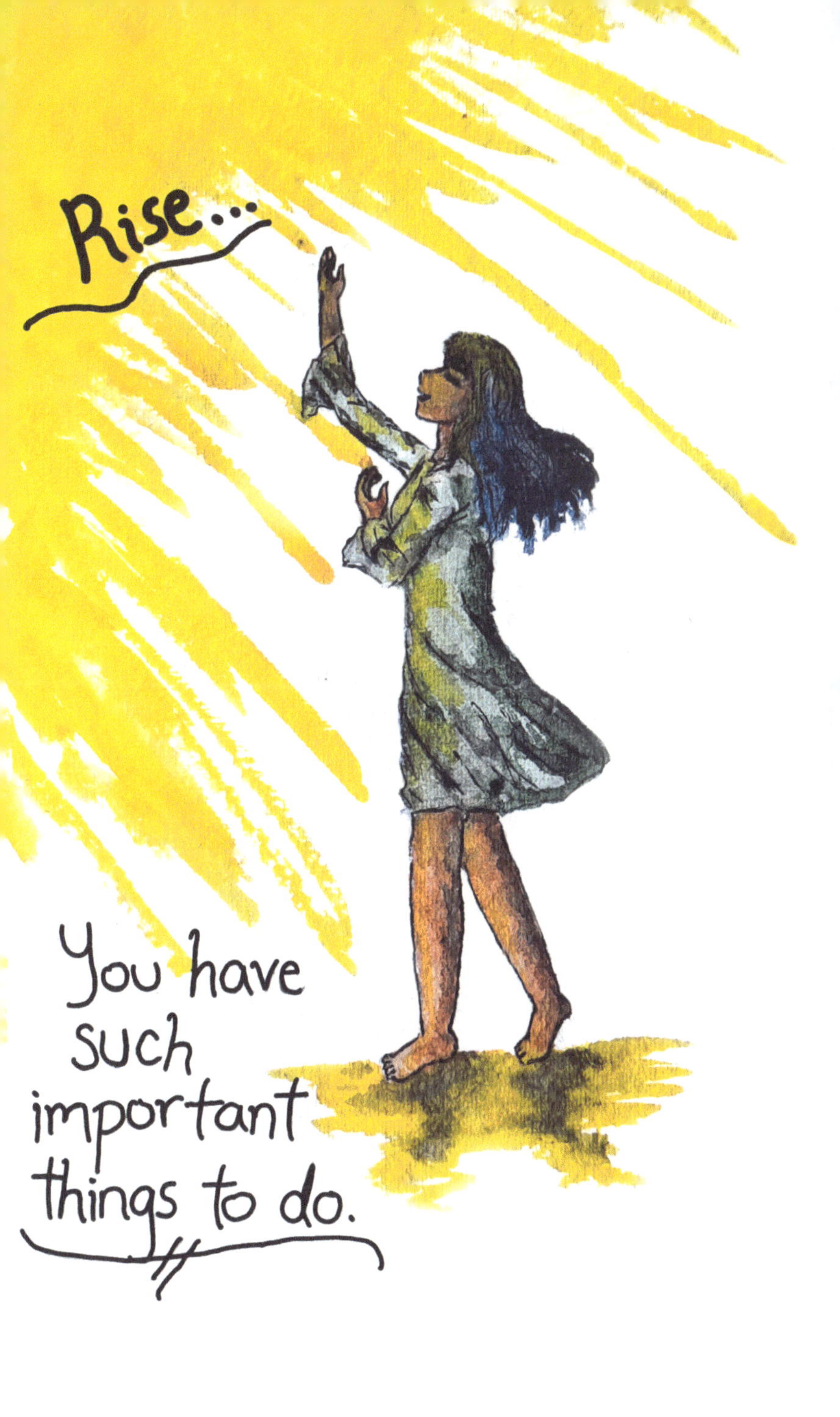
Rise...
You have such important things to do.

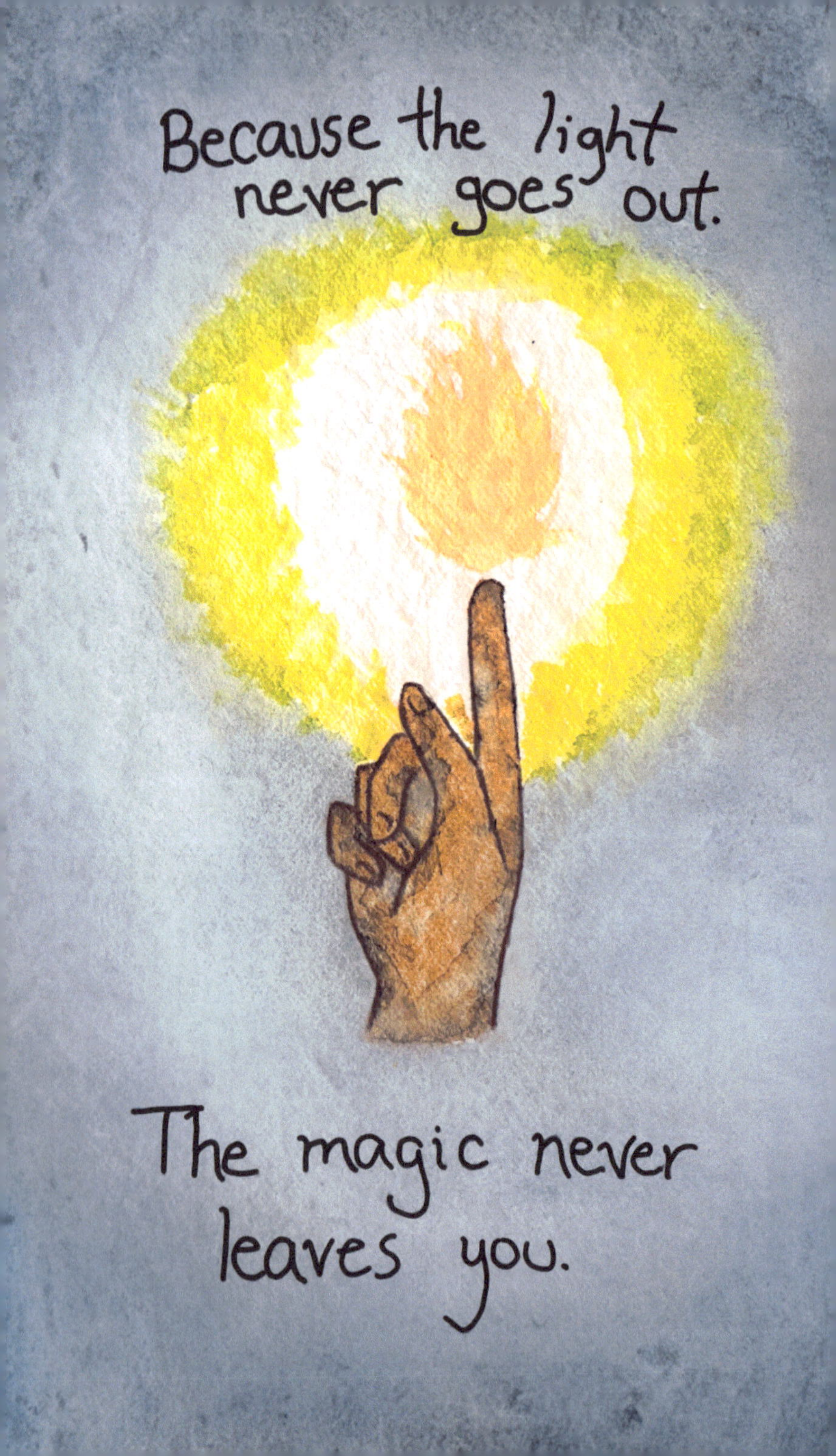
Because the light never goes out.
The magic never leaves you.

It only waits

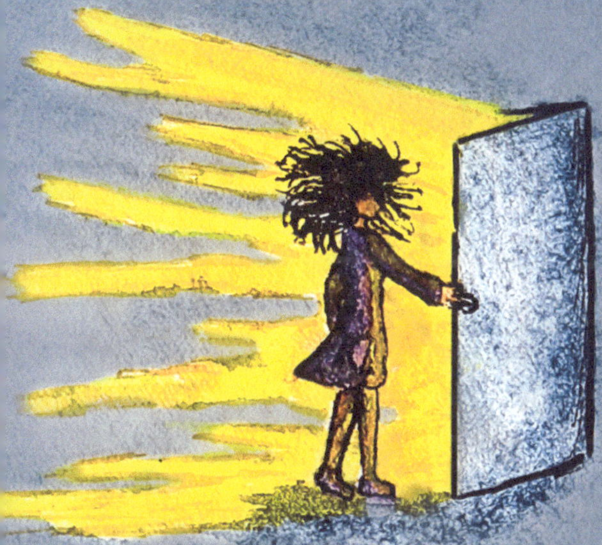

for you to return
to it again.

So let it
speak for you

in
kindness
and fire.

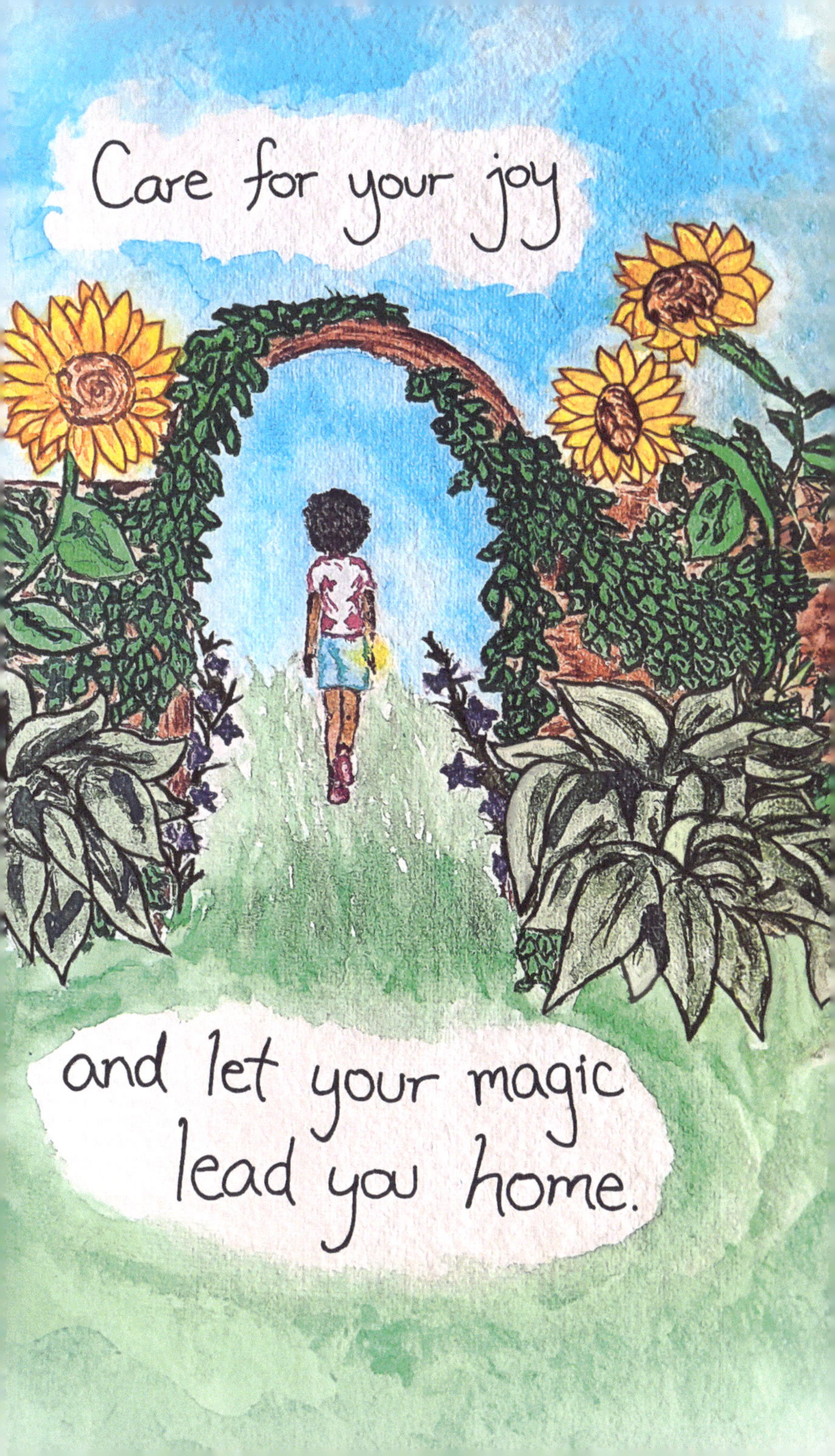
Care for your joy
and let your magic
lead you home.

I am so glad
you are here.

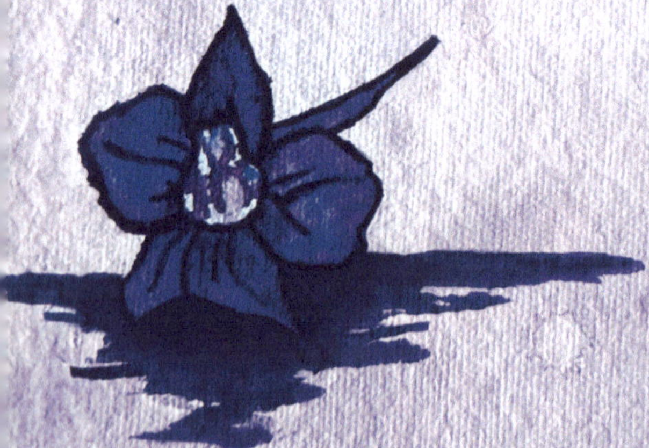

This book is just for you.
Thank you for picking it up.
I hope you got out of it exactly what you needed today.
I created this book during a difficult time in my life. I wanted it to be imperfect, a little chaotic the only way I know how to make art or anything else that matters.
I hope it inspires you to create your own beautiful, unique chaos.
I hope it reminds you that the more out of place you feel, the more magical you are.
There is so much in the world that is meant for you.
May you use your magic to find it and make all your dreams come true.

— Caitlin ♥

www.ingramcontent.com/pod-product-compliance
Ingram Content Group UK Ltd.
Pitfield, Milton Keynes, MK11 3LW, UK
UKHW061029310726
14089UKWH00007B/165
* 9 7 9 8 8 6 8 9 2 2 1 4 5 *